English-Dari-Persian Dictionary

Dr Yavar Dehghani

Introduction

Language is more than words. It is culture, identity, and the invisible architecture through which people understand themselves and each other. To speak a language is not merely to exchange information. It is to inhabit a particular way of seeing the world, shaped by centuries of history, geography, literature, and lived experience.

Persian is one of the world's great languages. With a literary tradition stretching back more than a thousand years, it has given the world the poetry of Rumi, Hafez, Saadi, and Khayyam, writers whose words have been translated into dozens of languages and read by millions of people who have never set foot in a Persian-speaking country. It is a language of extraordinary richness and precision, capable of expressing philosophical depth and emotional nuance with a concision that few languages can match.

Yet Persian is not one thing. Like all living languages, it has evolved differently in different places, shaped by local history, by contact with other languages, by the communities that have spoken it across centuries. Today, the two most widely spoken varieties of Persian are Farsi, spoken primarily in Iran, and Dari, spoken primarily in Afghanistan. These two varieties share the same ancient roots, the same script, and a large portion of their vocabulary and grammar. A speaker of Farsi and a speaker of Dari can generally understand each other. But the differences between them are real, significant, and frequently the source of confusion for learners, translators, and the communities themselves. This dictionary exists because of those differences.

The Relationship Between Farsi and Dari

Farsi and Dari are both direct descendants of Middle Persian, the language of the Sasanian Empire. When the Arab conquest of Persia in the 7th century CE brought Islam and the Arabic script to the region, Persian did not disappear. It absorbed, adapted, and re-emerged as New Persian, the language of poets, scholars, and administrators across a vast stretch of Central and South Asia. For centuries, this language served as the literary and administrative language of courts from Istanbul to Delhi. What we call Farsi and Dari today are the modern inheritors of that single classical tradition.

The divergence between them accelerated in the 19th and 20th centuries, as modern nation-states drew clearer boundaries and developed distinct national identities. Iran under the Qajar and Pahlavi dynasties undertook deliberate efforts to purify the language, replacing Arabic loanwords with words derived from Persian roots, and standardising vocabulary in ways that reflected an Iranian national identity. Afghanistan, whose Persian-speaking community had less exposure to these modernisation efforts and maintained stronger contact with classical Persian and neighbouring Turkic and South Asian languages, developed differently.

The result is a pair of languages that are closely related but not identical, like British English and Australian English, or Brazilian Portuguese and European Portuguese, but with differences that are in some areas more pronounced. A Farsi speaker arriving in Kabul will understand most of what they hear, but will encounter words, expressions, and pronunciations that are unfamiliar. A Dari speaker reading an Iranian newspaper will follow the text, but will notice that certain everyday words are different from the ones they use at home.

The Key Differences

The differences between Farsi and Dari fall into several main categories.

- *Vocabulary* is the most immediately noticeable. Many everyday words are simply different. Where Farsi says *māshin* (car), Dari may say *motar*. Where Farsi has adopted a modern Iranian neologism, Dari may have kept the older classical form, or borrowed from a different source altogether. This dictionary focuses primarily on these vocabulary differences, presenting the two variants side by side so that readers can see at a glance where the languages align and where they diverge.

- *Pronunciation* also differs significantly. Dari has preserved some sounds that have changed or disappeared in modern Farsi, notably the distinction between short and long vowels, and the pronunciation of certain consonants. The Dari spoken in Kabul sounds noticeably different from the Farsi spoken in Tehran, even when the words being used are the same. These pronunciation differences are not captured in written dictionaries, but they are an important part of what makes the two varieties distinct in practice.

- *Loanwords* reflect the different historical and cultural environments in which each variety developed. Farsi has absorbed significant vocabulary from French and other European languages, as well as from Russian, particularly in technical and administrative domains. Dari has been more influenced by Pashto, the other major language of Afghanistan, and has also borrowed from British English through the colonial period and subsequent international presence in Afghanistan.

- *Register and formality* can also differ. The system of politeness, the vocabulary used in formal versus informal contexts, and the conventions of written versus spoken language all show variation between the two varieties, sometimes in ways that can cause misunderstanding when speakers assume they are using shared conventions.

Who This Dictionary Is For

This dictionary has been compiled with several audiences in mind.

- *Translators* working between Farsi and Dari, or translating from English into either variety, will find it a practical reference for the moments when a word in one variety has no direct equivalent in the other, or when the apparent equivalent is misleading. The differences documented here are the differences that matter in professional translation, the ones where a Farsi-trained translator working on an Afghan text, or a Dari-trained translator working on an Iranian document, is most likely to make an error or miss a nuance.

- *Language learners* studying either Farsi or Dari will benefit from understanding how the language they are learning relates to its close relative. A learner of Farsi who encounters Dari speakers will be better prepared if they understand where the vocabulary differs. A learner of Dari who reads classical Persian literature will recognise how the language they are learning connects to one of the world's great literary traditions.

- *Community members*, members of the Iranian and Afghan diaspora communities, people with family connections to both countries, or those who work across these communities, will find the dictionary useful for navigating the linguistic differences that arise when communities whose languages are almost the same but not quite interact with each other.

- *Researchers, students, and educators* interested in Persian linguistics, comparative language study, or the history of the Persian language will find the dictionary a compact and accessible record of the contemporary differences between the two major varieties.

A Note on This Dictionary

The entries in this dictionary have been selected on the basis of practical utility, words and phrases that appear frequently in everyday communication, professional contexts, and public life. Priority has been given to entries where the Farsi and Dari equivalents differ, since it is precisely these differences that most reference works fail to document clearly. Where the two varieties use the same word, that word appears in both columns, providing useful confirmation for readers who may be uncertain whether a particular term is shared or variety-specific.

The dictionary presents entries in Persian script, which is used for both Farsi and Dari. Readers who are not familiar with the Persian script will find it useful to study the script alongside this dictionary, as the ability to read Persian script opens access to the full richness of both the Iranian and Afghan literary and cultural traditions.

This is not an exhaustive dictionary. The Persian language, in all its varieties, is vast, and no single volume could capture its full range. What this book offers is a practical, clearly organised, and linguistically informed starting point: a tool for understanding, comparison, and communication.

It is offered in the spirit of the languages themselves, in the hope that better understanding of the differences between Farsi and Dari will bring their speakers closer together, not further apart.

English	Dari	Persian
a parent with children	اولاد دار	بچه دار
a type of betting	عروس کشک	جناق شکستن
able	مستعد	توانا
ablution (wudu)	اودس	وضو
above	بالای	روی
absence	غیر حاضری	غیبت
academy	تولنه، آکادمی	فرهنگستان
accident	تصادم، قضا، تکر	تصادف
accommodation	تعمیر بودوباش، خانه رهایشی	ساختمان مسکونی، مسکن
accompany	کتی	همراه
accountability	مسئولیت	مسئولیت‌پذیری
accountant	محاسب	حسابدار
accounting	محاسبه	حسابداری
accounting chief	مدیر محاسبه	رئیس حسابداری
acquaintance	پیژندل شوی	آشنا
actions	اجراات	اقدامات
actor	اداکار، بازیگر	هنرپیشه
addict	نشه ئی	معتاد
administration	اجراات	تدابیر
administration office	اوراق	دفتر اداری
adoption	د پالنی اخیستل	فرزندخواندگی
advice, order	دایرکتیف	رهنمود
aeroplane	طیاره	هواپیما
afterlife	آخرت	آخرت
afternoon	پیشین، دیگر، مازدیگر	بعد از ظهر، عصر
agency	اجنسی	آژانس

agent	ایجنت		مامور
agreement	موافقه		توافق
air pollution	هوا ککرتیا		آلودگی هوا
airport	میدان هوایی، هوایی دگر		فرودگاه
alarm	آلارم		آژیر
alarm (clock)	شمته		زنگ ساعت
alcohol	الکول، شراب		مشروب، الکل
all together	کتله وی		دسته جمعی
almond	بادام		بادام
almost	تخمینا		تقریبا
also	هکذا		همچنین
aluminium	المونیم		آلومینیوم
always	تل		همیشه
anaesthesia	بیهوشی		بیهوشی
angel	ملک		فرشته
angina	آنجین		آنژین
angry	عصبی، قهر		عصبانی
animal farming	مالداری		دام داری
ankle	کونکل		قوزک
anniversary	سالیاد		سالگرد
annual	سالوار، کلنی		سالانه
antique	انتیک		عتیقه
anxiety	تشویش، اضطراب		اضطراب
any type	هر رنگه		هر نوع
appendix (organ)	آپندکس		آپاندیس
application / app	اپلیکیشن		برنامه
apprenticeship	ستاژ		کارآموزی
apricot	قیسی		زردآلو
aqueduct	کاریز		قنات

architect	مهندس	معمار
archive	آرشیف	آرشیو
area	ساحه	عرصه
area, size	مساحه	مساحت
argument	قیل و قال	قال و مقال
armature	آهن گول	آرماتور
army	اردو	ارتش
arrogance	ویار	غرور
art	آرت	هنر
artery	رگ	شریان
artificial intelligence	مصنوعي هوش	هوش مصنوعی
artist	ممثل	هنرمند
as	به حیث	به عنوان
ashamed / embarrassed	شرمیدلی	شرمنده
asphalt road	سرک قیر	راه آسفالت
assembly	جمعیت، اسامبله، جمیعت	مجمع
Assembly (material)	بسته کاری	مونتاژ
assets	مایملک	دارایی
assignment	مقرری	انتصاب
assistant	مرستیال	دستیار
associate professor	پوهنوال	استادیار
association	جمعیت	انجمن
asthma	دمه	آسم
at least	حداصغر	حداقل
athletic	سپورتی	ورزشی
attached to the letter	ضم مکتوب	پیوست نامه
attachment	منظمه، ضم	پیوست
attic	بالاخانه	زیر شیروانی
aunt (maternal)	خاله	خاله

English		
aunt (paternal)	تربور مور	عمه
automatic	اتومات	خودکار
automation	اتوماتیک سیستم	اتوماسیون
avalanche	برف کوچ	بهمن
awake	ویش	بیدار

English		
backpack	کولبار، خوله بکس	کوله پشتی
backyard	حویلی	حیاط
bag	خریطه، دستکول، بکس	کیسه، کیف، گونی
bakery	نان پزی	نانوایی
balance	پرتره	موازنه
balance (trade)	بیلانس	تراز
balcony	برنده	بالکن
bald	کل	کچل
balloon	پوقانه	بادکنک
banana	کیله	موز
bandage	بنداج	بانداژ
bank	بانک	بانک
barking	عف عف	واق واق
barracks	گارنیزون، قاغوش، قشله	پادگان
barrel	بیرل	بشکه
base	تهداب	پایه
basket	تکری	سبد
bat	موش پران، شب پرک	خفاش
bath house	غسلخانه	حمام
bath towel	جان خشکان	حوله حمام
bathing	جان شویی، غسل کردن	حمام کردن

battalion	کندک	گردان
battery	بالټی	باطری
beak	نول	منقار
beam (construction)	گادر	ستون
beans	فاسوله	لوبیا
beating	لت	کتک
beautiful	مقبول	زیبا
bed	کوچ، چپرکت	تخت
bed cover	سرجائی	روتختی
bedding	روجایی	ملافه
beef	غوشت غوا	گوشت گاو
beer	بیر	آبجو
beetroot	لبلبو	چغندر
being a creditor	ذمه گی	طلبکاری
believer	مؤمن	مؤمن
belly	خیړ	شکم
below	پایان	پایین
belt (car engine)	پتره	تسمه
bend (road)	گولایی	پیچ جاده
bended	چک	خمیده
Bible	انجیل	انجیل
bicycle	بایسکل	دوچرخه
big pot	تپ	تشت
bike	بایسکل	دوچرخه
bike rider	بایسکل سوار	دوچرخه سوار
bile	زرده	صفرا
bill	بل	قبض
biodiversity	ژوندي تنوع	تنوع زیستی
biography	سوانح	زندگینامه
biology	بیالوجی	زیست شناسی

English		
bird	مرغه	پرنده
birds	طیور	پرندگان
birth	تولدی	تولد
birth certificate	تذکره	شناسنامه
birth records office	اداره احصائیه	اداره ثبت احوال
birthday	روز تولدی	روز تولد
biscuit	کیک	بیسکویت
black	توره	سیاه
blackboard	تخته توره	تخته سیاه
bladder	پوقات	مثانه
blanket	کمپل	پتو
blinking	مژه بهم رساندن	چشم بهم زدن
blood	وینه	خون
blood pressure	فشار وینه	فشار خون
blue	شین	آبی
blueberries	سیاه چوب	ذغال اخته
boarding school	مکتب لیلیه	مدرسه شبانه روزی
body	جان	تن
body odour	ذفر	بوی زیر بغل
boiled	جوشانده	آب‌پز
bomb	بم	بمب
bombardment	بمبارد	بمباران
bone	هسکل	استخوان
bonesetter	تخته بند	شکسته بند
booking	ریزرف	رزرو
booth	غرفه	حجره
boots	موزه	چکمه
border	سرحد	مرز
border, margin	لبکی	حاشیه
boring	دق	دلگیر

boss	آمر	رئیس
bottle	بوتل	بطری
bottom (organ)	سرین	باسن
bow	غولک	کمان
bowl	تغاره	لگن
box	بکس	صندوق، جعبه
boxing	بکسینگ	بکس
boxing	بوکسینگ	مشت زنی
boy	بچه	پسر
bracelet	کره	دستبند
brain	دماغ سر	مغز
brake	بریک	ترمز
branch (tree)	نار	ساقه
bread	نان	نان
bread crumb	میده گی	خرده نان
break (car)	برک	ترمز
breakfast	نان صبح، ناشتا	صبحانه
breaking promise	بی لفظی	خلف وعده
breast	چچو	پستان
bribe	رشوت	رشوه
brick	خشت	آجر
bridge	پل	پل
brigade	لوا	تیپ
brigadier general	برید جنرال	سرتیپ
broadcast	برودکست	پخش
brooch	لاکت	سنجاق سینه
brother	ورور	برادر
brother's wife	ینگه	زن برادر
brown	نصواری	قهوه ای
bruise	سپین چرم	کبودی

English		
bubble	پوکانه	حباب
Buddhism	بودیزم	بودیسم
budget	بودیجه	بودجه
building	تعمیر، عمارت	ساختمان
bull	سرمنگسک	گاونر
bullet	پاغنده	گلوله
bullet shell	پوچک	پوکه
Bump (puddle)	چقوری سرک	دست انداز
burp	جشا	آروغ
bus	بس، سرویس	اتوبوس
bus stop	د بس استیشن	ایستگاه اتوبوس
business	کسب و کار	تجارت
busy	مصروف	مشغول
busy (crowded)	بیروبار	شلوغ
butcher	دارکش	جلاد
butter	مسکه	کره
by	ذریعه	بوسیله

English		
cabbage	کرم	کلم
cable	کیبل	کابل
cake	کیک	کیک
calendar	جنتری	تقویم
calf	چوچه گاو	گوساله
calm	آرام	آرام
camel	اشتر	شتر
camera	کمره	دوربین
camping	کمپ	اردو
canned	کانسرو	کنسرو
canteen	کانتین	بوفه
captain	تورن	سروان

Captain (pilot)	کپیتان	کاپیتان
car	موتر	ماشین
car boot	تولبکس	صندوق عقب ماشین
car wheel	تایر موتر	چرخ ماشین
carburettor	کاربیتر	کاربوراتور
card	پوچاق	کارد
cardamom	هل	هل
cardboard	کاغذ کاک	مقوا
cargo	کارگو	محموله
carpentry	ترکانی	نجاری
carpet	قالین	قالی
carrot	زردک	هویج
cart	گادی	گاری
cartridge (weapon)	کارتوس	فشنگ
case officer	کیس آفیسر	مامور پرونده
cat	پیشک	گربه
cauliflower	گلپی	گل کلم
ceasefire	اوربند	آتش بس
ceiling	چت	سقف
cellar	تاکوی	زیرزمین
cement pipe	بلول	لوله سیمانی
census	احصائیه نفوس	سرشماری
century	صدی	سده
cereal	سوجی	بلغور
certificate	سند	مدرک
chair	چوکی	صندلی
chalk	تباشیر	گچ
chandelier	قندیل	لوستر
change (money)	پول میده	پول خرد
change room	دریش کن	رختکن

English		
charge (an equipment)	چارج	شارژ
charge d'affaires	شارژدافیر	کاردار
charity	صدقه	صدقه
cheek	کومه	گونه
cheese	پنیر	پنیر
chemical	کیمیاوی	شیمیایی
chemical fertiliser	کود کیمیاوی	کود شیمیایی
chemistry	کیمیا	شیمی
cherry	شاه آلو	گیلاس
chess piece	گوت شطرنج	مهره شطرنج
chest (organ)	صندوق سینه	قفسه سینه
chewing gum	ساجق	آدامس
chick	چوچه	جوجه
chicken	چرگ	مرغ
chicken farm	فارم	مرغداری
chickenpox	آب چیچک	آبله مرغان
chickpeas	نخود	نخود
child	اشتک، طفل	بچه، کودک
child-like	اشتک واری	مثل بچه
childcare	ولکتون	مهد کودک
childhood	اشتکی، چوچه گی	بچگی، کودکی
childish	اشتکانه	کودکانه
childlike	اشتکانه	بچگانه
chimney	دودرو	دودکش
chin	الاشه، زنخدان	چانه
Chinese	چینائی	چینی
chives	گندنه	تره
chocolate	چاکلیت	شکلات
Christian	عیسوی	میلادی
Christianity	مسیحیت	مسیحیت

church	کلیسا	کلیسا
cigarette	سگرت	سیگار
cinnamon	دارچینی	دارچین
circular (office)	متحدالمال	بخشنامه
circumcision	ختان	ختنه
circumcision ceremony	ختنه	ختنه‌سوران
circus	سرکس	سیرک
citizen	هیوادوال	مقیم کشور
citizenship	تابعیت	شهروندی
citrus	سیتروس	مرکبات
city council	شاروالی	شهرداری
city district	کارته	ناحیه شهری
civil registration	د اسنادو ثبت	ثبت احوال
civilian	ملکی	غیر نظامی
class	صنف	کلاس
classmate	همصنفی	همکلاسی
classroom	صنف	کلاس درس
clay	گل ارمنی	خاک رس
clean	سچه	تمیز
clean water	آب سچه	آب تمیز
cleaner	خاکروب محافظ	نظافت چی
cleaning	پاک کاری، صفایی	پاک سازی، نظافت
cleric	روحانی	روحانی
climate change	د اقلیم بدلون	تغییر اقلیم
clock hand	ملخک	عقربه
cloud	وریځ	ابر
cloud (storage)	کلاود	فضای ذخیره‌سازی (ابر)
clover	شفتر	شبدر
club	کلب	کلوپ
coast	غاړه	ساحل

coat	بالاپوش	پالتو
coat hanger	کوت بند	رخت آویز
Cobra snake	چمچمه مار	مار کبرا
coconut	کوپره، ناریال	نارگیل
coffee	کافه	قهوه
cold	خنک	سرد
cold (illness)	زکام	سرماخوردگی
collar	یخن	یخه
colleague	اندیوال	همکار
colonel	دگروال	سرهنگ
coloured	رنگه	رنگین
comedy	کمیدی	کمدی
comma	کامه	ویرگول
command	قومانده	فرمان
commander	فوج دار	فرمانده
commercial warehouse	گدام تجارتی	انبار بازرگانی
commotion	های هوی	هیاهو
company	فرم	شرکت
company (army)	تولی	گروهان
compassionate	زړه سواندی	دلسوز
compatriot	وطن دار، وطنوال	هم وطن
compensation	تاوان	جبران
complaint	عریضه	شکایت
completely	بیخی	کاملا
complex	مغلق	پیچیده
compress	تربند	کمپرس
compressor	دمترک	کمپرسور
computer	کمپیوتر	کامپیوتر
concert	کانسرت	کنسرت

English		
concrete (construction)	سمنت	سیمان
concrete (material)	کانکریت	بتون
conditional mark	اشاره شرطی	علامت شرطی
condom	پوقانه	کاپوت
conference	کانفرانس	کنفرانس
confused	وارخطا	دستپاچه
confusion	وارخطایی	دستپاچگی
congress	کانگرس	کنگره
connection	کنکشن	اتصال
conscription	جلب عسکری	احضار به خدمت
constipation	قبضیت	یبوست
constitution	اساسي قانون	قانون اساسی
construction materials	مصالح تعمیراتی	مواد ساختمانی
consulate	قنسلگري	کنسولگری
contagious	ساری	مسری
contemporary	عصری	معاصر
contentment	زره خوشحالي	دلخوشی
contract	قرارداد	قرارداد
contraction	تعمیراتی	ساختمانی
cooking	پخلی کول	آشپزی
copy	کاپی	نسخه
copyright	معاش حق	حق مؤلف
core, stone	خسته	هسته
cork	کاک	چوب پنبه
corn	جواری	ذرت
corn (on feet)	زخه	میخچه
cornices	راد پرده	چوب پرده
coroner	قاضی تحقیق	پزشک قانونی
corrupt	چاپاتی	فاسد

corruption	فساد	فساد
cost	مخارج، مصارف	هزینه
cottage	کودلی	کلبه
cotton	پخته	پنبه
couch	کوچ	کاناپه
cough	کاسه	سرفه
council	جمعیت	شورا
country	هیواد	کشور
countryside	صیفیه	ییلاق
course	کورس	دوره تحصیلی
court	محکمه	دادگاه
cousin (paternal uncle's son)	تربور	پسر عمو
covered market	چته	بازار سرپوشیده
coward	ترسندوک	ترسو
coworker	سیال	همکار
crack	ترق، مویک	ترک، درز، شکاف
cracker	پتاقی	ترقه
crane	کرین	جرثقیل
cream	کریم	کرم
cricket	بمبیرک	جیرجیرک
crochet	جنگل دوزی	قلاب دوزی
crock	چاتی	خمره
crowded place	محل مزدحم	محل شلوغ
crumpled	چملک	مچاله
cucumber	بادرنگ	خیار
culture	کلتور	فرهنگ
cumin	جوشن	زیره
cupboard	الماری	کمد
cupping	کدوگک	بادکش

curious	کنجکاو	کنجکاو
currency	اسعار	ارز
curtain	کلکین	پرده
customs	گمرک	گمرک
cybersecurity	سایبري امنیت	امنیت سایبری

dairy products	شیریات	لبنیات
damage	تپ	زیان
dance	اتن، دانس	رقص
dancer	بازیگر	رقاص
dandruff	سبوسک	شوره
dark	خیره	تیره
dash	دش	خط تیره
daughter	لور	دختر
daughter-in-law	نزور	عروس
day and night	شبان روزان	شب و روز
deadline	ددلاین	ضرب‌الاجل
deaf	گنگ	کر
deaf & mute	گنگه	کر و لال
debt	دیبت	بدهی
deception	چم	فریب
decimal point	اعشاریه	ممیز
decision	فیصله	تصمیم
defendant	مدعی علیه	متشاکی
deforestation	د ځنګل له منځه وړل	جنگل‌زدایی
delay	تال	تاخیر
delay	تال	معطلی
delay	ځند	تاخیر
demonstration	مظاهره	تظاهرات
deposit (prepayment)	پیشکی	پیش پرداخت

English		
depression	افسردگـي	افسردگی
design	دیزاین	طرح
designing	دیزاین بندی	طرح ریزی
detergent	دترجنت	مواد شوینده
development program	پلان انکشافی	برنامه رشد
diabetes	دیابیت	دیابت
dictionary	دکشنری	لغتنامه
dietary restriction	پرهیز خوراکی	پرهیز غذایی
difficult	کورکی	سخت
digestive system	جهاز هاضمه	دستگاه گوارش
dill	شبت	شوید
dinner	نان شب	شام
dirt road	سرک خامه	جاده خاکی
dirty	چتل	کثیف
disability	معیوبیت	معلولیت
disappointed	سرددل	دلسرد
discipline	دسپلین	انضباط
discoveries	تفحصات	اکتشافات
discrimination	تبعیض	تبعیض
disgust	کرکه	انزجار
dish (kitchen)	برتن	ظرف
dismissal	برطرفي	اخراج
dissection	معاینات طب عدلی	کالبد شکافی
distance	مسافه	مسافت
divine decree	قضا او قدر	قضا و قدر
division	غند	هنگ
divorce	جلا کیدل	طلاق
dizziness	سرچرخی، سرگنس	سرگیجه
doctor	داکتر	دکتر
doctorate	داکتری	دکترا

document	سند	مدرک
documents	صکوک	اسناد
doll	گدی	عروسک
donna cover	شیت لحاف	رولحافی
donor	اعاده دهنده	اهدا کننده
doormat	گلیمچه	پادری
dorm	لیلیه	خوابگاه
dose	دوز	دوز
double shifts	دو وقته	دو شیفته
doubt	دلدلک	دودلی
download	داونلود	بارگیری
dowry (Islamic)	مهر	مهر
dozen	درجن	دوجین
drainage	زاه کشی	زهکشی
drama	درامه	درام
dramatic	دراموی	دراماتیک
drawer	روک	کشو
dried fruit	میوه خشک	خشکبار
drill	برمه	مته
driver	درایور، موتروان	راننده
driver's licence	لیسنس درایوری	گواهی رانندگی
driving	درایوری، موتروانی	رانندگی
driving licence	د درایوري جواز	گواهینامه رانندگی
drop (water)	چکه	قطره
drought	وچکالي	خشکسالی
dry bread	نان قاغ	نان خشک
duck	زاغابی	مرغابی
dumb	گنگس، تینگور، لوده	گنگ، نادان، خل
dummy	چوشک	پستانک
dustpan	بیلچه	خاک انداز

English		
earlobe	تکمه گوش، خاچ	نرمه گوش
earthen	کلالی، گلی	سفالی
earthenware	تیکر، کلال	سفال
earthquake	زلزله	زلزله
echo	توف	انعکاس صوت
eclipse	مهتاب گرفته گی	خسوف
eco	توف	پژواک
ecosystem	بیولوژیکی سیستم	اکوسیستم
edge	پل	لبه
edible	طعام	خوردنی
education (schooling)	تعلیمات	تحصیلات
education	تعلیم	آموزش
egg	هګۍ	تخم مرغ
eggplant	بادنجان سیاه	بادمجان
eggs	تخم	تخم مرغ
Eid al-Adha	لوی اختر	عید قربان
Eid al-Fitr	اختر	عید فطر
eight	اته	هشت
eighteen	هژده	هجده
elbow	هنجک	آرنج
election	تـاکنی	انتخابات
electric oven	داش برقی	اجاق برقی
electrical drill	برمه برقی	مته برقی
electrical power shortage	شارتی	اتصالی
electrician	برق والا	سیم کش
elephant	فل	فیل
eligible	مستحق	واجد شرایط

email		ایمیل	ایمیل
embassy		سفارت	سفارتخانه
emergency		عاجل	اورژانس
Emergency Department		دیپارتمنت ایمرجنسی	بخش اورژانس
emergency medicine		طب عاجل	طب اورژانسی
employee		کارمند	کارمند
employees		منسوبین	کارمندان
employer		مالک	کارفرما
empty		واک	خالی
endangered species		ښه منځه تلونکی ډول	گونه در خطر انقراض
engagement ring		شال انگشتر، چله	انگشتر نامزدی، حلقه
engine		انجین	موتور
engine		انجن	موتور
engineer		انجینر	مهندس
enrolment		راجستر	ثبت‌نام
environmental protection		د چاپیریال ساتنه	حفاظت از محیط زیست
epaulet		سرشانه	سردوشی
equipment		ماشینری، سامان	تجهیزات، لوازم
eraser		پنسل پاک	مدادپاکن
errand boy		چپراسی، پیاده	پادو
especially		خاصتا	بخصوص
ethics		کراکتر	اخلاق
ethnic		ملیتی	قومی
ethnicities		خیل و ختک	اقوام
evident		جلی	واضح
exam		امتحان	امتحان
excavation		برمه کاری	حفاری
excellent		کاکه	عالی

English		
excited	هیجاني	هیجان‌زده
excluded	مستثنی	به استثنا
excursion	چکر، میله، هواخوری	گردش
exhausted	مانده	خسته
exhausting	خسته کن	خسته کننده
exhaustion	ماندگی	خستگی
exhibition	نندارتون	نمایشگاه
expensive	قیمت	گران
expensiveness	قیمتی	گرانی
experimental	تجربوی	تجربی
expert, professional	مسلکی	متخصص
explosion	انفلاق	انفجار
explosives	مواد انفلاقی	مواد منفجره
express	تیزرفتار	سریع السیر
express post	داک چپاوی	پست فوری
extended family	لویه کورنی	خانواده گسترده
eyebrow	وروجن	ابرو
eyelash	برمژه	مژه

English		
fabric	تیکه	پارچه
fabric slates	سرگز	قواره پارچه
face to face	چشم به چشم	رویارو
factory	فابریکه	کارخانه
faculty	پوهنجی	دانشکده
fail	فیل	رد شدن
failed	فیل	ناکام
faith	ایمان	ایمان
fake	ناسره	قلابی
family by kinship	خسرخیل	فامیل سببی
famous	بنام	مشهور

English		
fan (cooler)	پکه	بادبزن
farm	مزرعه	مزرعه
farming	زراعت	کشاورزی
farming without water	للمی	دیمی
fart	چرنگ	گوز
fasting	روژه	روزه
fat	جور	چاق
father	بابه، پلار	پدر
father's brother's son	بچه کاکا	پسرعمو
fees	فیس	حق الزحمه
female	نسایی، اناث	زنانه، مونث
female long robe	چادری	چادر
fence	قطاره، کتاره	نرده
fertiliser	انبار	کود
fever	تبه	تب
fever reducing medicine	تب شکن	تب بر
fiancé	نامزد	نامزد
field of study	رشته	رشته تحصیلی
fig	انجیر	انجیر
fighter	جگار	ستیزه جو
file	فایل	فایل
file (document)	دوسیه	پرونده
film	فلم	فیلم
filming	فلم گیری	فیلم برداری
filter	صافه	صاف کن
finally	آخردست	بالاخره
fine (penalty)	جریمه	جریمه
finger	کلک	انگشت
fire	الو	آتش

English		
fire engine	موتر اطفائیه	ماشین اتش نشانی
fire extinguisher	آتش گل کن	کپسول آتش نشانی
fire incident	حریق	آتش سوزی
fire-fighters	اطفائیه	آتش نشانی
firework	شلیک احترام	آتش بازی
first	لمری	نخستین
first lieutenant	لمری بریدمن	ستوان یکم
fish	کب، ماهی	ماهی
fishing hook	چنگگ ماهی	قلاب ماهی گیری
fist	چپه	مشت
five	پنځه	پنج
flare	لمبه	شعله
flattering	چاپلوس	چاپلوس
flood	سیلاب	سیل
floor	تل	کف
floor (storey)	منزل	طبقه
flower	گل	گل
flu	ریزش	سرما خوردگی
fly replant	مگس پران	مگس کش
fold	قات	لا
folding	قاتکی	تاشو
food	خوراکه	خوراکی
food products	مواد ارتزاقی	مواد غذایی
foot heel	کوری پا	پاشنه پا
foot trace	پل	ردپا
for	درک	برای
forceps	سیخک	پنس
forefinger	انگشت شهادت	انگشت سبابه
forehead	چکاک	پیشانی
foreign language	ژبه بهرنی	زبان خارجی

foreman	آمرکار	سرکارگر
forest	جنگل	جنگل
fork	پنجه	چنگال
form	فورم، فرمه	فرم
fortune teller	فالبکاز	فالگیر
foundation	تهداب	اساس
fountain pen	خودرنگ	خودنویس
four	څلور	چهار
four corners	چهار کنج	چهار گوش
frame	چوکات، فریم	قاب
framework	چوکات	چهارچوب، قالب
freckles	شیرینکه	جوش صورت
free of charge	بلا عوض	رایگان
free of charge	بلا عوض	مفت
freedom of speech	د خبرو آزادي	آزادی بیان
freezing	یخبندی	یخبندان
fresh	تازه	تازه
fried	سرو	بریان
friend	اندیوال	دوست
friend	دوست	دوست
friendship	اندیوالی	دوستی
frog	بقه	قورباغه
frost	یخ	یخبندان
frozen	یخ زده	منجمد
fruit	میوه	میوه
fruit juice	آبمیوه	آبمیوه
fuel	روغنیات، محروقیات	سوخت
full	پوره	کامل
fun	ساعت تیری	تفریح
fundamental	تهدابی	اساسی

furniture	سامان خانه، فرنیچر	اثاثیه، مبلمان

gallbladder	تلخه	کیسه صفرا
gaming card	قطعه بازی	کارت بازی
garlic	سیر	سیر
gas	گیس	گاز
gas bottle	بالون گاز	کپسول گاز
gazebo	چپر	آلاچیق
gear box	گراری	چرخ دنده
gearbox	گیربکس	جعبه دنده
gearbox	گیر موتر	دنده ماشین
genealogy	نسب نامه	شجره نامه
general	عامه	عمومی
general manager	مدیر عمومی	مدیر کل
general plan	ماستر پلان	برنامه عمومی
general practitioner	داکتر فامیلی	دکتر عمومی
general staff	ارکان حرب	ستادکل
generous	بخبش‌نده	بخشنده
genitor	چوکی دار	دربان
geographical map	خریطه	نقشه جغرافیایی
geography	جغرافیه	جغرافیا
geology	جیالوجی	زمین شناسی
germ	مکروب	میکروب
German measles	سرخکان جرمانی	سرخچه
Germany	جرمنی	آلمان
gillyflower	قرنفل	گل میخک
ginger	ادرک	زنجبیل
girder	آهن گادر	تیرآهن
glass (cup)	گلاس	لیوان
glazier	آئینه بر	شیشه بر

global warming	د خُمکي گـرميدل	گرم شدن کره زمين
globule	کرويات	گلبولها
glorious	شاندار	با شکوه
glutton	خفک	دله
goal keeper	گلکيپر	دروازه بان
God	خدای / الله	خدا / الله
golden	زرين	طلايی
goods	امتعه	کالا
gourmet, stew	سالند، قورمه	خورش
government	دولت	دولت
governor	والی، گورنر، قوماندان	استاندار، فرماندار
grade	نمره	نمره
grandchild	لمسی	نوه
grandfather	نيکه	پدربزرگ
grandmother	بی بی کلان	مادر بزرگ
grape	انگـور	انگور
grapefruit	چکوتره	گريپ فروت
grass	واښه	علف
grateful	مننه‌منونکی	سپاسگزار
grater	ملی تراش	رنده
gravel	جغله	سنگ ريزه
green	زير شين	سبز
green tea	چای شين	چای سبز
greeting	احوال گيری	احوال پرسی
grenade	بم دستی	نارنجک
grey	بور، خر	خاکستری
grinder	پلاس	گاز انبر
grocery market	مندهی	بازار مواد خوراکی
group	گروپ	گروه
growth	انکشاف	رشد

guarantee	گرانتی	ضمانت
guardian	سرپرست	سرپرست
guarding	ترصد	حراست
guesthouse	مسافرخانه	مسافرخانه
guillemot	ناخنک	گیومه
guilt	گناه احساس	احساس گناه
gum (organ)	بیره	لثه
gutter	ناوه	ناودان
gutty	شکمبو	شکمو
gynaecologist	داکتر نسائی	دکتر زنان
gypsy	جت	کولی

haggling	جگړه	چانه زنی
hail	ژاله	تگرگ
hair lock	چوتی	گیسو
Hajj (pilgrimage)	حج	حج
halal (permissible)	حلال	حلال
hallway	دهلیز	راهرو
hammer	میخکوب	چکش
hand gun	تفنگچه	هفت تیر
hand writing	نسخه قلمی	دست خط
happiness	خوشبختي	خوشبختی
happy	خوشحاله	شاد
haram (forbidden)	حرام	حرام
hard	گورکی	سفت
hardware	هاردویر	سخت‌افزار
hastily	هله گک، تریله	با عجله
hatred	نفرت	نفرت
health	صحت، روغتیا، حفظ الصحه، جانجوری	بهداشت، سلامتی

health inspector	روغتیاوال	بازرس بهداشت
health related	صحی	بهداشتی
healthy	جور	سلامت
heart	دل	قلب
heat exhausted	جل زده	گرما زده
heaven	جنت	بهشت
heaviness	ثقل	سنگینی
heavy	گرنگ، ثقیل	سنگین
heavy industries	صنایع ثقیل	صنایع سنگین
hedgehog	خارپشت	جوجه تیغی
heel	تخماق	پاشنه
height	قداندام	قد
helicopter	هلیکوپتر	هلیکوپتر
helix	تارپیچ	مارپیچ
hell	دوزخ	جهنم
helmet	کلاه فولادی	کلاه خود
henna	خینه	حنا
herbal shop	بنجاره گی، بنیه گری	عطاری
herbalist	بنجاره	عطار
herd	پاده	گله
here and there	لر و بر	این طرف و آن طرف
hiccups	هکک	سکسکه
hidden	پت	مخفی
hide and seek	چشم پتکان	قایم موشک
high court	ستره محکمه	دادگاه عالی
high heel	کوری بلند	پاشنه بلند
high pitch	صدای تربم	صدای زیر
high school	لیسه	دبیرستان
higher education	تعلیمات عالی	تحصیلات عالی
highway	شاهراه	بزرگراه

English		
hill	غندی	تپه
Hinduism	هندویزم	هندوئیسم
history	تاریخ	تاریخ
holding (a function)	تدویر	برگزاری
hole	دفه	سوراخ
holidays	رخصتی	تعطیلات
holy book	مقدسه کتاب	کتاب مقدس
homeless	بی سرپناه	بی خانمان
homework	کورنی دنده	تکلیف
hook	چاپوز، پتره	قلاب، گیره
hookah	چلم	قلیان
hoopoe	شانه سرک	شانه به سر
hoot	هارن کردن	بوق زدن
hopeful	هیلمن	امیدوار
hopeless	مایوس	ناامید
horn	هارن	بوق
horse power	هارس پاور	اسب بخار
horsefly	غورمگس	خرمگس
hose	پایپ	شنلک
hospital	شفاخانه	بیمارستان
hostage	یرغمال	گروگان
hot water bag	مشکوله	کیسه آب گرم
hot water system	بایلر	آبگرمکن
hotel	هوتل	هتل
hour	بجه، ساعت	ساعت
house painting	سفید چونه	نقاشی ساختمان
How are you?	جوری؟	خوبی؟
human rights	د بشر حقونه	حقوق بشر
humanity	علوم بشری	علوم انسانی
hundred	سل	صد

hurry up	هله	زودباش
husband	شوی	شوهر
husbands of sisters	باجه	باجناق
husband's brother	ایور	برادر شوهر
husband's father	خسر	پدرشوهر

ice cream	آیس کریم، شیر یخ	بستنی
idea	مفکوره	ایده
identification documents	اسناد هویتی	مدارک شناسایی
ill	خسته، ناجور	بیمار
illiterate	بی‌سواد	بی‌سواد
illness	ناجوری	بیماری
imam	امام	امام
immunisation	وقایه سازی	ایمن سازی
impatient	بی‌حوصله	بی‌حوصله
in love	مینه‌وال	عاشق
including	بشمول	شامل
income	عاید	درآمد
indifferent	بی‌تفاوته	بی‌تفاوت
Indomitable	سرزور	سرکش
Inevitably	لاچار	ناچار
infection	انفکسیون	عفونت
Infertile	سترون	نازا
inflation	انفلاسیون	تورم
influenza	زکام	آنفولانزا
information	معلومات	اطلاعات
inheritance	ترکه	ارثیه
injection	پیچکاری	تزریق
injured	افگار	زخمی

ink	رنگ قلم	مرکب
innocent	بی قصور	بی تقصیر
insect	حشره	حشره
inside out	سرچپه	برعکس
insomniac	بیدارخواب	بی خواب
instead of	متبادل	به عوض
Insulation materials	کاغذ فیر	عایق ایزوگام
insulator	انسولیتر	عایق
intellectual	منور	روشنفکر
internet	انترنیت	اینترنت
intersection	چهار راهی، چوک	چهار راه
intestine	روده	روده
invoice	بیجک، بیل	فاکتور
involved parties	جوانب ذیسهم	طرف های درگیر
Islam	اسلام	اسلام
island	تاپو	جزیره
issue	قضیه	مسئله

jack	تایرکش	جک
jacket	کرته، کرتی	کاپشن، کت
jam	مربا	مربا
janitor	خانه سامان	سرایدار
January	جنوری	ژانویه
Japan	جاپان	ژاپن
Jar	تیکر	کوزه
jar,	جگ	تنگ آب
Jasmine	چمبیلی	یاسمن
jealous	حسد	حسود
jelly	جیلی	ژله
jewellery	زیورات	جواهرات

English		
Jewish	جهود	یهودی
job application	غوښتنلیک کاري	درخواست کار
job interview	انترویو	مصاحبه کاری
joke	فکاهی	جوک
joking	مذاق	شوخی
journalist	نامه نگار، خبریال	خبرنگار، گزارشگر
journey	سفر	سفر
Judaism	یهودیت	یهودیت
judge	قاضي	قاضی
jumper (clothes)	جمپر	پولور
justice	عدالت	عدالت

English		
kebab	کباب	کباب
kettle	چاینک، چایجوش	قوری، کتری
key	کلی	کلید
key holder	کلی بند	جاکلیدی
kick	پس لگدی	اردنگی
kidney	گرده	کلیه
kind	مهربانه	مهربان
king	باچا	پادشاه
kite	کاغذپران	بادبادک
knee	توله پای، زنگون	زانو
knee cap	عینک زانو	کاسه زانو
knowledge	پوهنه	دانش
knowledgeable	پوهند	دانا

English		
label	لیبل	برچسب
laboratory	لابراتور	آزمایشگاه
lake	بحیره	دریاچه
lamb	غوشت پسه	گوشت گوسفند
land	ځمکه	زمین

English		
landing of stairs	زینه خانه	پاگرد پله
landlord	خانه والا	صاحب خانه
language	لسان	زبان
laptop	لپتاپ	لپتاپ
late	ناوخته	دیروقت
late	ناوخت	دیر
later on	پسان تر	بعدتر
lawyer	وکیل	وکیل
laxative	قبض گشا	مسهل
leader	لیدر	رهبر
leaders	اراکین	سران
leaking ceiling	چکک	چکیدن سقف
leave	رخصتی	مرخصی
lecture	لکچر	سخنرانی
lecturer	پوهنیار	دانشیار
leech	جوک	زالو
left handed	چپه دست	چپ دست
lender	تیکه دار	اجاره دهنده
lens	عدسیه	عدسی
lentil	دال نخود، نسک	عدس
lentils	مسور	عدس
lesson	سبق	درس
letter	مکتوب، خط	نامه
letterhead	برگه	سربرگ
library	کتابتون	کتابخانه
licence	لایسنس	جواز
licence (permit)	جواز	مجوز
lieutenant	بریدمن	ستوان
lieutenant colonel	دگرمن	سرهنگ دوم
lift	لفت	آسانسور

light globe	گروپ	لامپ
light industries	صنایع خفیف	صنایع سبک
light switch	ساکت	کلید برق
lighter	لایتر	فندک
like	واری	مثل
lime (construction)	چونه	آهک
line	لاین	خط
lip stick	لب سرین	ماتیک
liquid	آبکی	مایع
list	لست	لیست
literacy	سواد	سواد
literate	خواننده	باسواد
literature	ادبیات	ادبیات
little boy	بچگگ	پسر بچه کوچک
live broadcast	مستقیم نشر	پخش زنده
liver	جگر	کبد
living	گزاره	زندگی
living condition	گزاره	شرایط زندگی
living style	سویه زندگی	سطح زندگی
lizard	چلپاسه	مارمولک
loan	قرضه	وام
lock	قلف	قفل
lonely	زره تنگ	دلتنگ
long	کشال	دراز
long term program	پلان طویل المدت	برنامه دراز مدت
longing	حسرت	حسرت
loss	ضرر	ضرر
loudspeaker	لودسپیکر	بلندگو
love	مینه	محبت
luck	چانس	شانس

lucky	طالع‌مند	خوشبخت
luggage	سامان سفر	بار سفر
lullaby	له لو	لالایی
lunch	نان چاشت	ناهار
lung	شش	ریه

machine	ماشینری	ماشین
machine gun	ماشیندار	مسلسل
madam	بادار، میرمنه	سرکارخانم
magazine	مجله	مجله
major	جگرن	سرگرد
major general	تورن جنرال	سرلشکر
make up	فیشن	آرایش
male	ذکور	مذکر
manager	منیجر	مدیر
mandarin	سنتره، کینو	نارنگی
manual	طرزالعمل	دستورالعمل
map	نقشه	نقشه
marble game	تشله بازی	تیله بازی
market	مارکیت	بازار
market	بازار	بازار
market square	چوک	میدان بازار
marketing	مارکیتنگ	بازاریابی
marriage certificate	نکاح خط	سند ازدواج
marriage contract	نکاح	عقد
mask	ماسکه	ماسک
mason	معمار	بنا
mass	کتله	توده
massage	ماش	ماساژ
massive	کتله، گوت	انبوه

master	مستر	اوستا
master's degree	ماستری، اسپیرانتوری	فوق لیسانس
mat	بوریا	حصیر
matches	گوگرد	کبریت
materials	مصالح	مواد
maternity leave	رخصتی زیږون	مرخصی زایمان
maternity ward	ژیزنتون	زایشگاه
mathematics	ریاضی	ریاضی
maximum	حداعظم	حداکثر
mayor	شاروال	شهردار
measles	سرخکان	سرخک
measurement	سایز گیری	اندازه گیری
measuring tape	فیته اندازه گیری	نوار اندازه گیری
meat broth	شوربا	آبگوشت
meat grinder	ماشین گوشت	چرخ گوشت
mechanic	ماشین کار، میخانیک	مکانیک
medical pipe	بول دانی	لوله طبی
medicine	ادویه	دارو
meeting	درسن، جلسه	ملاقات، جلسه
melon	خربوزه	طالبی
menstruation, period	عادت ماهوار	عادت ماهانه
mental	دماغی	ذهنی
menu	مینو	لیست غذا
messenger	ایلچی	قاصد
metal bars	آهن گول	میل گرد
metal sheet	آهن تخته	آهن ورق
metals	آهن باب	آهن آلات
meter	میتر	کنتور
method	میتود	روش
middle school	مذُغنی ښوونځی	مدرسه راهنمایی

midnight	د شپې نیمه	نیمه شب
midwife	قابله	ماما
military	عسکری	نظامی
military commander	دلگی مشر	فرماندار نظامی
military service	خدمت عسکری	خدمت سربازی
military training centre	لیسه عسکری	آموزشگاه نظامی
milk	شیدی	شیر
mill	جلندی	آسیاب
mine (material)	کان	معدن
mine (pronoun)	از من	مال من
mineral water	منرل واتر	آب معدنی
minister	وزیر	وزیر
minister's assistant	قلم مخصوص	دستیار وزیر
ministry	وزارت	وزارت
minute	دقیقه	دقیقه
miracle	معجزه	معجزه
missing	لادرک	مفقود الاثر
mistake	غلطی	اشتباه
misunderstanding	غلط فهمی	سوء تفاهم
mixed	گد	مخلوط
mobile	داینمیک	متحرک
mocking	تتره، تتربو	مسخره
molar tooth	دندان کرسی	دندان آسیا
money	پیسه	پول
money exchange centre	چینج	صرافی
money saving	پاسره	ذخیره پول
monkey	شادی	میمون
month	میاشت	ماه

English			
monthly		ماهوار	ماهانه
monuments		آبدات	آثار
moral principles		قواعد سلوک	اصول اخلاقی
morning		صباح	صبح
morning		سهار	صبح
mosque		جومات	مسجد
mother		مور	مادر
motorcycle		موتور سایکل	موتور سیکلت
mould		گوژ	کپک
mountain		غر	کوه
mountain climbing		کوه گردی	کوهنوردی
mountaineer		کوه گرد، کوه پیما	کوهنورد
mourning		ماتم	عزاداری
moustache		بروت	سبیل
mowing lawn		قطع کردن چمن	زدن چمن
Mr		شاغلی	جناب اقا
mud		خامه	خاکی
mud		خټه	گل و لای
mufti (Islamic scholar)		مفتي	مفتی
mule		مرکب	قاطر
municipality		شاروالي	شهرداری
muscle		ماهیگگ	ماهیچه
muscle		گوشت	ماهیچه
museum		میوزیم	موزه
music		موسیقي	موسیقی
mustard		مصتر	خردل

English			
nail (finger)		نوکان	ناخن
nail (tools)		کوکه	میخ

English		
nail polish	رنگ ناخن	لاک
naked	لچ	لخت
napkin	دست پاک	دستمال
narrow	تنگ	باریک
narrowness	ضیق	تنگی
national	ولسی	ملی
national airline	هوانوردی ملکی	هواپیمایی کشوری
national council	ولسی جرگه	شورای ملی
national ID card	د هویت کارت	کارت ملی
naughty	بلاگک	بازیگوش
nausea	دل بدی	تهوع
nausea	دلبدی	تهوع
necessary	بکار	لازم
neck	غاړه	گردن
needle hole	دفه سوزن	سوراخ سوزن
neighbour	گاوندی	همسایه
net	جال	تور
network	جالی	توری
never	هیڅکله	هرگز
news	خبر	خبر
newspaper	اخبار، جریده	روزنامه
next	پسین	بعدی
next to	به اتصال	جنب
NGO	غیردولتي اداره	سازمان غیردولتی
night	شپه	شب
nightly	شپی	شبانه
nine	نهه	نه
nomad	کوچی	کوچ نشین
non-believer	کافر	کافر
non-cash assets	جایداد	دارایی غیر منقول

noon	چاشت	ظهر
noon	غرمه	ظهر
Norway	نوروی	نروژ
note	خط، پرزه	یادداشت
note (bank)	بانک نوت	اسکناس
notebook	کاپی	دفتر
now	فعلا	الان
now	اوس	الان
nuclear	ذروی	هسته ای
nuclear explosion	انفلاق ذروی	انفجار هسته ای
nuclear family	کوچنی کورنی	خانواده هستهای
number	لمبر، نمبر	نمره، شماره
number plate	نمبر پلیت	شماره ماشین
nurse	نرس، همشیره	پرستار
nursing	نرسینگ	پرستاری
nursing home	مرستون	خانه سالمندان
nuts and bolts	نت و بولت	پیچ و مهره

occupation	حرفه	شغل
offer, suggestion	آفر	پیشنهاد
office	آفس	دفتر
often	اکثراً	اغلب
oil	غوري	روغن
oil (petroleum)	تیل خاک	نفت
old	پخته سال	پیر
Old (thing)	داغمه	کهنه
old woman	سرسفید	پیرزن
old woman	سابونه	زن پیر
older brother	آکه، لالا	برادر بزرگ

English		
on (as in light or engine)	چالان	روشن
on call doctor	داکتر نوکریوال	دکتر کشیک
one	یو	یک
one hundred thousand	لک	صد هزار
onion	پیاز	پیاز
only	صرف	فقط
opinion	مفکوره	عقیده، نظر
opium	افیون	تریاک
orange	نارنجي	نارنجی
orange (fruit)	کینو، مالته	پرتقال
order	فرمایش	سفارش
orphan	بی پدر	یتیم
orphanage	یتیمخانه	پرورشگاه
ovary	تخمدانی	تخمدان
oven	داش	اجاق
overtime	اضافي کار	اضافه کاری
oxygen	اکسیجن	اکسیژن
o'clock	بجه	ساعت

English		
pacific ocean	بحرالکاهل	اقیانوس آرام
packing	پکینگ	بسته بندی
painter	رنگمال	رنگ کار
palm	تلی	پنجه
pan	کرایی	تابه
pantyhose	سلدراج	جوراب شلواری
paper	قرطاس	کاغذ
paper pin	الپن	پونز
parachute	پراشوت	چتر نجات
parade	رسم گذشت	رژه

parcel	پارسل	بسته پستی
parenthesis	قوس	پرانتز
parking	پارکینگ	پارکینگ
parliament	پارلمنت	پارلمان، مجلس
parrot	توتا	طوطی
parties of the deal	بیع پار	طرف معامله
partridge	زرک	کبک
party, celebration	میله	جشن
pass	پاس	قبولی
pass cards	کارت دخول به طیاره	کارت ورود به هواپیما
passage	کوتل	گردنه
passenger car	موتر تیزرفتار	ماشین سواری
passport	پاسپورت	گذرنامه
password	شفر	رمز عبور
pastry shop	کلچه فروشی	قنادی
pasture	علفچر	چراگاه
paternity leave	رخصتي پلاري	مرخصی پدری
patient	صبرلرونکی	صبور
pattern	پاتن	الگو
payment	تادیه	پرداخت
peace	سوله	صلح
peace (tranquillity)	سکون	آرامش
peach	شفتالو	هلو
peak	تالاق	قله
pear	ناک	گلابی
peas	دال	نخود
pedal	پایدل	پدال
pen	قلم	خودکار
pencil	پنسل	مداد
pencil	قلم	مداد

pencil sharpener	پنسل تراش	مداد تراش
peninsula	جزیره نما	شبه جزیره
pension fund	د تقاعد صندوق	صندوق بازنشستگی
people	ولس	مردم
pepper	مرچ	فلفل
per kilo	تولګی	کیلویی
performance review	کاري ارزیابی	ارزیابی عملکرد
perfume	کولونیا	ادوکلن، عطر
period (menstruation)	عادت ماهوار	قاعدگی
permit	جوازنامه، منظوری	مجوز
personal details	تفصیلات شخصی	جزئیات فردی
personality	اوتوریته	شخصیت
petrol	پترول	بنزین
petrol tank	مخزن تیل	باک بنزین
petrol tank	تانک تیل	پمپ بنزین
pharmacy	ادویه فروشی	داروخانه
phone	تیلفون	تلفن
photography	فوتوگرافي	عکاسی
physical education	ورزش	درسی (ورزش)
physics	فزیک	فیزیک
physiotherapy	فیزیوتراپی	فیزیوتراپی
pickle	اچار	ترشی
picnic	پکنیک	پیک نیک
piece	توته، چیره، تلم، پاغنده	پاره، تکه، قاچ
piety	تقوا	تقوا
piggy bank	غولک	قلک
pilgrimage	زیارت	زیارت
pillow	بالشت	بالش
pillowcase	پوش بالشت	روبالشی
pilot	طیاره ران، پیلوت	خلبان

pilot cabin	کبین پیلوت	کابین خلبان
pinch	چندی	نیشگون
pink	گلابی	صورتی
pipe	نل	لوله
pipeline	پایپ لاین	خط لوله
pit	چقور	چاله، گودال
pity	ترحم	ترحم
plain (desert)	بیابان	دشت
plan	مسوده	طرح
plane fuel	محروقات طیاره	سوخت هواپیما
plant	بوتی	گیاه
planting tree	شاندن درخت	کاشتن درخت
plants	نباتات	گیاهان
plaster	پلستر	گچ
plaster work	گل کاری	گچ کاری
plaster worker	گل کار	گچ کار
plastering (bone)	پلستر کول	گچ گرفتن
plate	پلیت	پلاک
plate (dish)	قاب، رکابی	بشقاب
platform	میز خطابه	منبر
playing in the snow	برف جنگی	برف بازی
pliers	انبور	انبر
plot	سکیم	نقشه
plough	قلبه	شخم
ploughing	قلبه کشی	شخم کاری
plum	آرغنج	آلو
plumbing	نلدوانی	لوله کشی
Plummet	شاول	شاغول
pneumonia	سینه بغل	سینه پهلو
podcast	پودکست	پودکست

point of view	ساحه دید	دیدگاه
poisoning	زهر خوردن	مسموم شدن
pole	فیلپایه	تیر
police	پولیس	پلیس
police station	ماموریت پولیس	اداره پلیس
policy	پالیسی	سیاست
political bureau	بیروی سیاسی	دفتر سیاسی
political party	سیاسي گوند	حزب سیاسی
politician	سیاست وال	سیاستمدار
polygamist	انباقدار	مرد دوزنه
pomegranate	انار	انار
poor (in money)	غریب	فقیر
population	نفوس	جمعیت
port	پورت	بندر
porter	جوالی	باربر
post	پسته	پست
post box	بکس پوسته	صندوق پستی
post card	پست کارد	کارت پستال
post office	پوسته خانه	پستخانه
postman	پسته رسان	نامه رسان
pot	چری	دیگ
potato	کچالو	سیب زمینی
power pole	چراغ پایه	تیر چراغ برق
power station	استیشن	نیروگاه
pram	گادی	کالسکه
prayer (Islamic)	نماز، دعا، لمونځ	دعا، نماز
prayer mat	جای نماز	سجاده
precent	فیصد	درصد
pregnant	حامله دار	حامله
preparation	تکه کاری	تهیه

English		
prescription	نسخه	نسخه
presence	حاضری	حضور و غیاب
presentation	پریزنتیشن	ارائه
president	رئیس جمهور	رئیس‌جمهور
primary school	ښوونځی	مدرسه ابتدایی
prime minister	صدراعظم	نخست‌وزیر
priming	گلگل	بتونه کاری
principal	آمر	مدیر مدرسه
principles	پرنسیپ	اصول
print	طبع	چاپ
printing shop	مطبعه	چاپخانه
priority	اولیت	اولویت
prison	بندی خانه	زندان
privacy	شخصي محرميت	حریم خصوصی
process	پروسه	روند
produce	پیداوار	محصول
producer	تکه کار	تهیه کننده
production	پیداوار	تولید
professional	مسلکی	تخصصی
professor	پوهنوال	استاد
profit	منافع	سود
program	پروگرام، پلان	برنامه
project	پروژه	پروژه
promotion	ترقي	ترفیع
propaganda	پروپاگاند	تبلیغ
proposal	خسرونی	خواستگاری
prosecution office	سارنوالی	دادستانی
prosecutor	سارنوال	دادستان
prostitute	جافۀ	فاحشه
protest	پروتست	اعتراض

proud	متکبر	مغرور
province	ولایت	استانداری
provision	تمویل	تامین
psychology	سایکالوجی	روانشناسی
published materials	نشرات	نشریات
pulley	پیچک	قرقره
pumpkin	آشکدو	کدو
punishment	جزا	تنبیه
pupil (organ)	ننی گگ	مردمک چشم
puppy	چوچه سگ	توله سگ
purple	بادنجانی، سوسنی	بنفش
pus	ریم	چرک
pyjamas	دریشی خواب	پیژامه

quean	غر	بدکاره
questionnaire	انگت	پرسشنامه
quick	تیز، عاجل	تند، زود
quiet	چوپ، خاموش	ساکت
quince	بهی	به
Quran	قرآن کریم	قرآن
radiator	ردیتر	رادیاتور
radio	ریدیو	رادیو
radiography	اکسریز	رادیو گرافی
radish	ملی سرخک	تربچه
railway	خط ریل	راه آهن
rain	بارش	باران
rainbow	کمان رستم	رنگین کمان
rainy	برساتی	بارانی
raisin	کشمش	کشمش
Ramadan	رمضان	رمضان

rank	رتبه	درجه
raspberry	راسبری	تمشک
razer	پل ریش	تیغ
ready	تیار	آماده، حاضر
real estate agent	اجنت رهنمای معاملات	بنگاه معاملات ملکی
reason	پلمه	دلیل
receipt	بل	رسید
recipe	طرزالعمل	دستور پخت
record	ریکارد	رکورد
recorder	تیپ ریکاردر	ضبط صوت
recording	ریکارگیری	ضبط
records office	تحریرات	دفتر اداره
recreational trip	سیلانی	مسافرت تفریحی
recycling	ریسایکلینگ	بازیافت
red	سور	قرمز
red cross	سره میاشت	هلال احمر
reduction	تقلیل	کاهش
referee	ریفری	داور
reforms	ریفورم	اصلاحات
refugee	کدوال	پناهنده
registered letter	مکتوب راجستری	نامه سفارشی
registration	راجستر	ثبت
registration fee	فیس راجستر	هزینه ثبت
regression	پس ماندگی	عقب ماندگی
regretful	پشیمانه	پشیمان
regularly	لاینقطع	بطور منظم
regulator	دیسپچر	تنظیم کننده
reinforced concrete	کانکریت آهن دار	بتون آرمه
relative	خپلوان	خویشاوند
relatives	اقارب	خویشاوندان

English		
relaxation	آرامی	راحتی
religious endowment	وقف	وقف
religious leader	ملا	ملا / آخوند
renewable energy	تجدیدیدونکي انرژي	انرژی تجدیدپذیر
rent	ته جایی	کرایه
repair	ترمیم	تعمیر
repentance	توبه	توبه
report	راپور	گزارش
republic	جمهوریت	جمهوری
request	استعلام	درخواست
research	سروی	پژوهش
research	تحقیق	تحقیق
reservation	رزرو	رزرو
reservoir	تانک	منبع
residence	بودوباش	اقامت
residence	محل بودوباش، محل رهایش	محل زندگی، محل سکونت
residency	اقامت	اقامت
resident	باشنده	ساکن، مقیم
residential	رهایشی	مسکونی
residential place	ملکیت	محل مسکونی
resignation	استعفا	استعفا
responsibility	ضمه	مسئولیت
responsible person	مسئول	مسئول
restaurant	رستورانت	رستوران
retailer	پرچون فروش	خرده فروش
retirement	تقاعد	بازنشستگی
return	عودت	برگشت
ribs	قبرغه	دنده
rice	برنج	برنج

rice pilaf	پلاو	پلو
rich	پیسه دار	ثروتمند
ring finger	انگشت بینام	انگشت حلقه
ritual bath	غسل	غسل
river	دریا	رود
road	وات	جاده
robot	انسان میخانیکی	روبات
robotics	روبوتیک	رباتیک
rock	کاڼي	صخره
rocket launcher	راکت انداز	موشک انداز
roof insulation	کاغذ تارکول	عایق بام
room	کوټه	اتاق
rose	گل گلاب	گل سرخ
rotten	گنده	گندیده
round	ګول	گرد
route	لار	مسیر
row	قطار	ردیف
rubber	رابر، لاشتک	لاستیک، کش
rubbish	زباله	آشغال
rule of law	د قانون حاکمیت	حکومت قانون
run on gas	غازی	گازی
rural police station	تهانه	پاسگاه
rust	مورچانه	زنگ فلز

sabotage	سابوتاژ	خرابکاری
sad	جگرخون، خفه	غمگین
saddle	پاردم	زین
safe (container)	سیف	گاوصندوق
safe	مصئون	امن
safety	مصونیت	امنیت

saffron	جادی، زعفران	زعفران
salad	سلاد	سالاد
salary	معاش	حقوق
sales	لیلامی	حراجی
saliva	خیو	آب دهن
salt	مالگه	نمک
sand	کاغذ ریگمال	سنباده
sand	شگه	شن
sandals	کروی، نالی	نعلین
saucer	رکابی	نعلبکی
sausage	ساسیج	سوسیس
scaffolding	خوازه	داربست
scared	ویرهلی	ترسیده
scattered	تیت	پراکنده
scene, stage	ستیج	صحنه
scholarship	بورس، اسکالرشیپ	بورسیه
school	مکتب	مدرسه
school janitor	چپراسی مکتب	مستخدم دبستان
school principal	مدیر ښوونځی	مدیر مدرسه
science	ساینس	علوم
scientist	پوهندوی	دانشمند
scientists	پوهان	دانشمندان
scratch	پرت	خراش
screw (tools)	بولت	پیچ
screw driver	پیچکشی، پیچ تاو	پیچ گوشتی
sea	بحر	دریا
seat	سیت	صندلی
seatbelt	سیفتی بیلت	کمربند ایمنی
second	ثانیه	ثانیه
second lieutenant	دوهم بریدمن	ستوان دوم

secondary	ثانوی	متوسطه
secondary education	تعلیمات ثانوی	تحصیلات متوسطه
secretary	منشی، سکرتر	دبیر، منشی
secretly	پټ پټ	مخفیانه
section	بلوک	دسته نظامی
sector	سکتور	بخش
sedan car	تیزرفتار	سواری
seed	کلچه	دانه
semester, term	سمستر	ترم
seminar	سیمینار	سمینار
senior	مشر	ارشد
senior expert	پوهنیال	کارشناس ارشد
server	سرور	سرور
settlement (residence)	مسکن گزینی	اسکان
seven	اووه	هفت
sewing machine	ماشین خیاطی	چرخ خیاطی
sexual relation	امور مباشرتی	رابطه جنسی
shake	جنگه	تکان
shameless	دیده درای	بیحیا
shell	مین	خمپاره
shepherd	پاده وان	چوپان
ship	بیړی	کشتی
shoemaker	بوت دوز	کفاش
shoes	بوت	کفش
shooting	فیر، گلوله باری	تیراندازی
shop	دوکان	فروشگاه
short	قصیر	کوتاه
short (height)	قدپخش، پخچک	کوتاه قد
short term program	پلان قصیرالمدت	برنامه کوتاه مدت
short-sighted	کمبین	نزدیک بین

shortness of breath	نفس تنگی	تنگی نفس
shoulder	راشبیلک	کتف
shoulder	اوزه	شانه
shovel	راشبیل	پارو
shower	شاور	دوش
sick leave	رخصتي مريضي	مرخصی استعلاجی
siege	بلوکاد	محاصره
sign	سرلوحه، اشاره	تابلو، علامت
signboard	بورد	تابلو
silkworm	پیله	کرم ابریشم
silver	سپین‌زری	نقره‌ای
sin	گناه	گناه
single	تاق	تک
sink	تپ دستشویی	دست شویی
sir	صاحب	آقا
siren	هارن	سوت
sister	خور	خواهر
sister in law	زن ایور، ننو، خیاشنه	جاری، خواهر شوهر، خواهر شوهر
sister's husband	یازنه	شوهر خواهر
six	شپر	شش
size	سایز	اندازه
skein	کلاوه	کلاف
ski	سکی	اسکی
skilled	چیره دست	ماهر
skin	جلد	پوست
skin	جلد	پوست
skull	پوزه‌ی سر	جمجمه
sky	اسمان	آسمان
slap	شپلاق	سیلی

sledgehammer	پلوک	پتک
slippers	چپلک	دمپایی
slippery	لشم	لیز
slope	اوترایی	سرازیری
sludge	غریژن	لجن
small district	مکروریان	ناحیه کوچک شهری
small	میده	خرد، ریز
smallpox	چیچک	آبله
smartphone	سمارت فون	گوشی هوشمند
smoothness	زازل	صافی
smuggler	قاچاقبر	قاچاقچی
snoring	غژغژ	خروپف
snow	واوره	برف
snow ball	توپ برفی	گلوله برف
social media	توولنیزه شبکه	شبکه اجتماعی
sofa	بازودار	مبل
soft drink	کولدرینک	نوشابه
software	سافتویر	نرم‌افزار
solar	لمریز	خورشیدی
solder	لیم	لحیم
soldering	لیم کاری	لحیم کاری
soldering tool	کاوه	هویه
sometimes	یگان وقت	گاهی
son	زوی	پسر
son-in-law	زوم	داماد
soon	عنقریب	به زودی
soon	ژر	زود
soul (foot)	تل	کف پا
soul	روح	روح
soup	شوربا	سوپ

English		
sour cherry	آلوبالو	آلبالو
souvenir	سرراهی	سوغاتی
spare	فالتو	زاپاس
spare part	پرزه	یدک
spare parts	پرزه جات	لوازم یدکی
speciality	مسلک	تخصص
spectator	تماشا بین	تماشاگر
speed	سرعت	سرعت
speedometer	سپیدومیتر	سپیدومتر
spell (magic)	تعویذ	طلسم
spice	مساله	ادویه
spider web	تار جولا	تار عنکبوت
spinach	پالک	اسفناج
spinal cord	حرام مغز	نخاع
spinning top	فرفرانک	فرفره
sponge	ابر	اسفنج
sponger	تیارخور	مفت خور
sponsor	سپانسر	اسپانسر
sport	سپورت	ورزش
spouse	خاوند / بنځه	همسر
spring (metal)	سپرنگ	فنر
spring (water)	سرچینه	چشمه
sprinkled	پاشان	پاشیده
spy	اجنت	جاسوس
squad	دلگی	جوخه
square	چهار کنج	مربع
staff	ارکان	ستاد
stairs	زینه	پله، نردبان
stale bread	نان قاغ، نان باسی	نان بیات
stammered	تتله	الکن

English	Dari/Persian	Dari/Persian
stamp (letter)	تکت پوستی	تمبر
stamp	تاپه	مهر
station	استیشن	ایستگاه
stationary	قرطاسیه	نوشت افزار، لوازم التحریر
statistics,	احصائیه	آمار
steering wheel	اشترنگ	فرمان ماشین
step (kin)	اندر، ناسکه	ناتنی
step brother	برادر سکه، برادر عینی	برادر تنی
stick	دانگ	چماق
stingy	خسیس	خسیس
stitches / sutures	سلاخی	بخیه
stomach	معده	معده
stool (chair)	چارپایی	چارپایه
stool	مواد غایطه	مدفوع
storage	ذخیره	ذخیره‌سازی
storm	خاکباد	بوران، طوفان
strawberry	توت زمینی	توت فرنگی
strawberry	مرینه	توت فرنگی
stream	شاخه سیند	رود
street	سرک	خیابان
stress	فشار	استرس
stripes	خط دار	راه راه
student (school)	شاگرد	دانش‌آموز
student (university)	محصل	دانشجو
student in charge	خلیفه، کفتان	مبصر کلاس
student number one	اول نمره	شاگرد ممتاز
students	متعلمین	شاگردان
study	مطالعه	مطالعه

stupid	تپنگوز	احمق
style	سان	طرز
Subject	مضمون	درس
subsidence	ترسب	فرونشینی
sugar	بوره	شکر
suit	دریشی، کرتی و پتلون	کت و شلوار
suitcase	جامه دانی، بکس	چمدان
sulphur	سلفر	گوگرد
sunburn	جل	آفتاب زدگی
sunburned	جل زده	آفتاب زده
sunflower	آفتاب پرست	آفتابگردان
sunset	آفتاب نشست	غروب
supervisor	نگران	ناظر
supply	اکمالات	تدارک
supporter	پالندوی، ساتندوی	پشتیبان، حامی
surgery	عملیات، آپریشن	عمل جراحی
surname	تخلص	نام خانوادگی
surprised	حیران	متعجب
survey	سروی	تحقیق
swamp	دلدل	باطلاق
swear word	داو	فحش
sweat	خوی	عرق
sweets	کلچه	شیرینی
swimming	آب بازی	شنا
swing	گاز	تاب
switchboard	سویچ بورد	مرکز تلفن

English		
T-shirt	بوشارت	پیراهن آستین کوتاه
table	دسک	میز
tablet	گولی، تابلیت	قرص
tar	تارکول	قیر
tarantula	غندل	رتیل
tax	مالیه	مالیات
tax office	مستوفیت	اداره مالیات
tax official	تحصیلدار	مامور مالیات
tax	تکس	عوارض
taxi	تکسی	تاکسی
teacher	معلم	معلم / مدرس
teacher training	دارالمعلمین	دانشسرا
tear (eye)	آبدیده	اشک
technical workshop	ورکشاپ	کارگاه فنی
technician	تخنیک دان	تکنیسین
technique	تخنیک	تکنیک
television	تلویزیون	تلویزیون
temple	معبد	معبد
ten	لس	ده
ten million	کرور	ده میلیون
tenant	کرایه نشین	مستاجر
tent	خیمه	چادر
tertiary student	محصل	دانشجو
testimony	شاهدی	شهادت
textbook	کتاب درسی	کتاب درسی
the day after	پس صبا	پس فردا
theatre	تیاتر، ننداری	تاتر
therapeutical	معالجوی	درمانی
thesis	تیزس	پایان‌نامه
thick	دبل	ضخیم، کلفت

English		
thick soup	آش	آش
thin	مهین	نازک
third lieutenant	دریم بریدمن	ستوان سوم
thousand	زر	هزار
thread and needle	تار و سوزن	نخ و سوزن
three	دری	سه
three hundred	سه صد	سیصد
throat	گلون	گلو
thugs	لوچک	اوباش
thumb	انگشت کلان	شست
thunder	الماسک	برق
thunder and lightning	ورعد	رعد و برق
Thursday night	جمعه رات	شب جمعه
thyroid	تیرویید	تیرویئد
ticket	تکت	بلیط
tie	نیکتایی	کراوات
tight	کورکی	محکم
tile	کاشین	کاشی
time	کرت	دفعه
tin	چست	حلبی
tin	قلعی	قلع
tin roof	آهن پوش	شیروانی آهنی
tip (money)	بخششی	انعام
tired	ستومانه	خسته
title deed	د ملکیت سند	سند مالکیت
to accept	قبولدار بودن	قبول داشتن
to answer	ځواب ورکول	جواب دادن
to applaud	چک چک	کف زدن
to arrest	قید کردن	دستگیر کردن
to ask	پرسان کردن	پرسیدن

to attach	پیوست کردن	پیوستن
to be amazed	کلیگک شدن	مبهوت شدن
to be annoyed	خفه شدن، دق شدن	آزرده شدن، رنجیدن
to be beaten	لت خوردن	کتک خوردن
to be late	تال خوردن	دیر کردن
to be obliged	مکلف بودن	مجبور بودن
to be on call	نوکری کردن	کشیک کشیدن
to beat	لت کردن	کتک زدن
to bite	چک زدن	گاز گرفتن
to borrow	به عاریت گرفتن	قرض گرفتن
to brush	برس زدن	مسواک زدن
to bury	گور کردن	فرو کردن
to butt	تکر زدن	شاخ زدن
to buy	اخیستل	خریدن
to catch flu	خنک خوردن	سرما خوردن
to celebrate	تجلیل نمودن	جشن گرفتن
to charge	چارج کول	شارژ کردن
to cheat in a deal	تپ زدن	گول زدن در معامله
to chopped	توته کردن	خرد کردن
to clean	صفا کردن، پاکول	تمیز کردن، پاک کردن
to close	بند کردن، بسته کردن	بستن
to close	بندول	بستن
to come	راتلل	آمدن
to compare	سر دادن	مقایسه کردن
to complete (a form)	خانه پری	پر کردن
to compress	تکر کردن	کمپرس کردن
to cook	پخلی کول	آشپزی کردن
to cope	جور آمدن	کنار آمدن
to copy	کاپی کول	کپی کردن

to crash	تکر خوردن	تصادف کردن
to cry	ژړل	گریستن
to cut in pieces	تلم تلم	قاچ قاچ
to dance	دانس کردن	رقصیدن
to deceive	چل دادن	فریب دادن
to decide	فیصله کردن	تصمیم گرفتن
to delete	دیلیت کول	حذف کردن
to dial	دایل کردن	شماره گرفتن
to do cupping	کدوگک نشاندن	بادکش انداختن
to do errands	پیاده گی	پادویی
to draw	قرعه بازی	قرعه کشی
to drink	څښل	نوشیدن
to drown	دوپ شدن	غرق شدن
to eat	خوړل	خوردن
to end	انجام یافتن	تمام شدن
to fall	افتیدن	افتادن
to fart	تیزیدن، گوز زدن	گوزیدن
to find	یابیدن	یافتن
to finish	ختمول	تمام کردن
to fold	قات کردن	تا کردن
to get fuel	تیل گیری	سوخت گیری
to get lost	مفقودی	گم شدن
to get sick	ناجور شدن	بیمار شدن
to give	ورکول	دادن
to give birth	زاد کردن	زائیدن
to give directions	لار ښودل	راهنمایی کردن
to glow	برقک زدن	برق زدن
to go	تلل	رفتن
to hate	کرکه لرل	نفرت داشتن
to have breakfast	ناشتا کردن	صبحانه خوردن

to help	مرسته کول	کمک کردن
to hide	پت شدن	مخفی شدن
to hold breath	نفس قید کردن	نفس نگه داشتن
to ignore	شانه گگ زدن	بی اعتنایی کردن
to inspect	تلاشی کردن	تفتیش کردن
to install	انستال کول	نصب کردن
to joke	مذاق کردن	شوخی کردن
to know	معرفت داشتن	شناختن
to laugh	خندل	خندیدن
to leak	چلک کردن	چکیدن
to learn	زده کول	یاد گرفتن
to leave	ماندن	گذاشتن
to like	خوش داشتن	دوست داشتن
to listen	اوریدل	گوش دادن
to live alone	یوازی ژوند کول	تنها زندگی کردن
to lock	قفل کول	قفل کردن
to lose (financial)	تپ خوردن	زیان کردن
to lose	ورکول	گم کردن
to lose weight	وزن باختن	وزن کم کردن
to love	مینه لرل	دوست داشتن
to make a mess	چرک کردن	کثیف کردن
to make a mistake	خطا کردن	اشتباه کردن
to measure	قد اندام گرفتن	اندازه گرفتن
to mix	گد کردن	قاتی کردن
to move (houses)	کوچ کشی	اسباب کشی
to move, to shake	شور خوردن	تکان خوردن
to offer	پاس کردن	پیشنهاد کردن
to open	خلاصول	باز کردن
to park	پارکنگ کردن	پارک کردن
to participate	سهم گرفتن	شرکت کردن

to pass (moving)	تیر کردن	رد کردن
to pass (exam)	کامیاب شدن	قبول شدن
to pass (time)	تیر کردن	گذراندن
to peel a chicken	چندی کردن	پرکندن مرغ
to place	ایښودل	قرار دادن
to plant	نشاندن	کاشتن
to play	لوبه کول	بازی کردن
to plough	شیاریدن، قلبه کردن	شخم کردن
to polish	پالش کردن	صیقل دادن
to pop	ترقاندن	ترکاندن
to press	پچق کردن	فشار دادن
to print	طبع کردن	چاپ کردن
to pull	کش کردن	کشیدن
to push	تیله کردن، جپ خوردن	هل دادن
to put petrol	تیل گیری	بنزین زدن
to read	لوستل	خواندن
to receive	اخیستل	گرفتن
to record	ریکاردگیری کردن	ضبط کردن
to remember	یاددهانی کردن	یادآوردن
to repair	جور کردن	تعمیر کردن
to return	پس آمدن	برگشتن
to return (something)	بازگرداندن	پس دادن
to return	راستنیدل	بازگشتن
to return (something)	بیرته ورکول	برگرداندن
to rub	تپه کردن، شکیدن	مالیدن
to run	منډه وهل	دویدن
to sack	سبکدوش کردن، برطرف کردن	اخراج از کار
to save	سیو کول	ذخیره کردن

to scan	سکین کول	اسکن کردن
to seal	سرغچ کردن	پلمپ کردن، مهر و موم کردن
to search	پالیدن	جستجو کردن
to see	لیدل	دیدن
to sell	پلورل	فروختن
to send goods	بارچالانی	فرستادن کالا
to send something	روان کردن	فرستادن چیزی
to set	تاله کردن	چیدن
to shake	تکاندن	تکان دادن
to sit	ښستن	نشستن
to sleep	ویده کیدل	خوابیدن
to slip	لخچیدن، تکر خوردن	لغزیدن، لیز خوردن
to solve	فیصله کردن	حل کردن
to sprain	مچ خوردن	پیچ خوردن
to squish	شبلیدن	چلاندن
to stand	ایستاد شدن	ایستادن
to start	پیل کول	شروع کردن
to stop	پرچو کردن	متوقف کردن، ایستادن
to store	گدام کردن	انبار کردن
to submit	تحویل دهی	تسلیم کردن
to suck	چوشیدن	مکیدن
to supervise	نگرانی کردن	نظارت کردن
to swear	داو زدن	فحش دادن
to swing	گاز خوردن	تاب خوردن
to take	اخیستل	برداشتن
to take notice	غور کردن	دقت کردن
to take off clothes	لباس کشیدن	لباس درآوردن
to talk	گپ زدن	صحبت، حرف زدن، کردن

English		
to teach	زده کول / ښودل	یاد دادن
to tear	چیر کردن	پاره کردن
to think	چرت زدن	فکر کردن
to thread	تار کردن	نخ کردن
to tighten	چپرپیچ کردن	محکم بستن
to travel	سفر کول	سفر کردن
to trick	چپ دادن	گول زدن
to tune	طیون کردن	کوک کردن
to turn off	گل کردن، بند کول	خاموش کردن
to turn on	خلاص کول	روشن کردن
to turn on the car	چالان کردن	روشن کردن ماشین
to turn on the light	بل کردن	روشن کردن چراغ
to understand	پوهیدل	فهمیدن
to urinate	بول کردن	ادرار کردن
to wait	انتظار کول	انتظار کشیدن
to wake up	پاڅیدل	بلند شدن
to walk	روان کیدل	راه رفتن
to wash hands	لاسونه مینځل	دست شستن
to watch	سیل کردن	تماشا کردن
to wear	اغوستل	پوشیدن
to welcome	پیشوایی کردن	استقبال کردن
to whistle	اشپلاق کردن	سوت زدن
to win	کمایی شدن	برنده شدن
to wink	ابروگک کردن	چشمک زدن
to work	کار کول	کار کردن
to write	لیکل	نوشتن
tobacco	تمباکو	توتون
today	نن	امروز
together	یکجا	باهم
toilet	تشناب	توالت

English		
toilet seat	کمود	صندلی توالت
tomato	بانجان رومی	گوجه فرنگی
tomorrow	سبا	فردا
tonsil	تانسیل	لوزه
tool	آله	آلت
tools	سامان	ابزار
toothbrush	برس دندان	مسواک
tooth grinding	دندان قرچک	دندان قروچه
toothpaste	کریم دندان	خمیر دندان
to fertilise	انبار دادن	کود دادن
Torah	تورات	تورات
total	سرجمع	مبلغ کل
tourism	تورزم، سیاحت	جهانگردی، گردشگری
tourist	تورست	جهانگرد
tournament	تورنمنت	دوره مسابقات
towel	روی پاک	حوله
town	مینه	شهرک
toy	سامان بازی	اسباب بازی
trachoma	کوکره	تراخم
trade	دادوگرفت	دادوستد
trade union	کارگري اتحادیه	اتحادیه کارگری
traditional	عنعنوی	سنتی
traditional medicine	داروی عنعنوی	طب سنتی
traditions	عنعنات	آداب و رسوم
traffic	ارشه درشه	رفت و آمد
traffic accident	ترافیکي پیښه	تصادف
traffic light	ترافیک لایت	چراغ راهنما
traffic lights	اشاره، چراغ ترافیکی	چراغ راهنمایی
traffic sign	لوحه ترافیکی	تابلوی رانندگی
traffic signs	اشارات ترافیکی	علامات ترافیکی

train (transport)	ریل	قطار
train station	د ریل استیشن	ایستگاه قطار
training	تعلیمی، تربیوی	آموزشی، تربیتی
translator	ترجمان	مترجم
transparency	شفافیت	شفافیت
transport	ترانسپورت	وسیله نقلیه
trap	جال، تلک	دام
tray	پنتوس	سینی
treatment	تداوی	درمان
treaty	تړون	معاهده
tree	ونه	درخت
trench	مرچل	خندق
Tribunal	دیوان	دادگاه
trick	چم	حیله
trousers	پتلون	شلوار
trousseau	جهاز	جهیزیه
trowel	پشنجه	ماله
truce	روغ	آشتی
truck	لاری	کامیون
truck driver	لاری والا	راننده کامیون
trumpet	ترم	شیپور
trunk	غوله	کنده درخت
tuberculosis	توبرکلوز	سل
tuition fee	فیس	شهریه
tumour	تومور	غده
tunnel	تونل	تونل
turkey	فیلمرغ	بوقلمون
turmeric	ورمیاسپه	زردچوبه
turquoise	فیروزه	فیروزه
turtle	سنگ بقه	لاک پشت

English		Pashto	Dari
twenty		شل	بیست
twin		دوگانه	دوقلو
two		دوه	دو
twofold		دو قات	دو لا
two hundred		دوصد	دویست
type of rug		شطرنجی	جاجیم
typhoid		محرقه	حصبه
typist		تایپیست	ماشین نویس
tyre		تایر	لاستیک

English		Pashto	Dari
umbrella		چتری	چتر
uncertain		تنکیر	نامعلوم
uncle (maternal)		ماما	دایی
uncle (maternal)		خالو	دایی
uncle (paternal)		تره	عمو
uncommitted		غیر منسلک	غیر متعهد
underground water		آبهای تحت الارضی	آبهای زیرزمینی
underwear		خراته، چوته	زیرپیراهن، شورت
unemployment insurance		بیمه بیکاري	بیمه بیکاری
unfortunate		بدبیار	بدشانس
uniform		بالاپوش، فورم	روپوش، یونیفورم
United Nations		ملګري ملتونه	سازمان ملل
university		پوهنتون	دانشگاه
university entrance exam		کانکور	کنکور
university president		ریاست پوهنتون	ریاست دانشگاه
unripe		نارس	کال
update		اپدیت	بهروزرسانی
upload		اپلود	بارگذاری

urgent	عاجل	فوری
urine	پیشاب	ادرار
usage	چالاندن	بهره برداری کردن
uterus	بچه دان	رحم

vaccine	واکسین	واکسن
vagina	چوز	فرج زن
vain	چتی	بیهوده
valley	وادی	دشت، دره
valuable	قیمت دار	گران بها
vase	گلدانی	گلدان
vegetable oil	تیل نباتی	روغن نباتی
vegetables	سبزیجات	سبزیجات
vehicle	موتر	خودرو
vehicles	عراده جات	اتومبیل ها
verbal	تقریری	شفاهی
vest	واسکت	جلیقه
veterinarian	وترنر	دامپزشک
veterinary	وترنری	دامپزشکی
victorious	بریالی	پیروز
vinegar	سرکه	سرکه
visa	ویزه	ویزا
visit	لیدنه	بازدید
vocal cords	اوتار صوتی	تار های صوتی
volcano	اور غر	آتشفشان
vote	رای	رأی
wage	اجوره، تنخواه، اجوره	اجرت، دستمزد، مزد
waist	ملا	کمر
wait	باش	صبر کن
walker	پای دوانک	روروک

wall socket	وال ساکت	پریز
wallet	بکس دستی، بکس جیبی	کیف دستی
walnut	چارمغز	گردو
war	جگړه	جنگ
warehouse	تحویل خانه، دیپو	انبار
warehouse handling	موجودی	انبارگردانی
warehouse keeper	تحویلدار	انباردار
warhead	کلاگگ	کلاهک
washing machine	کالا شویی	لباس شویی
watch maker	ساعت والا	ساعت ساز
watching	سیل	تماشا
watchman	پیره دار	نگهبان
water pipe	نل آب	لوله آب
water pollution	اوبه ککرتیا	آلودگی آب
water pomp	واترپمپ	پمپ آب
water sprinkler	بانتی	آبپاش
waterfall	د اوبو لویدل	آبشار
watermelon	تربوز	هندوانه
wave	ستونک	موج دریا
website	ویبسایت	وبسایت
wedding	توی	عروسی
wedding	واده	عروسی
wedding dress	لباس تویانه	لباس عروسی
week	اوونی	هفته
weekly	هفته وار	هفتگی
welding	ولدنگ کاری	جوشکاری
welfare officers	افسران رفاه عامه	مأمورین رفاهی
western toilet	کمود	توالت فرنگی
wet	زاه	مرطوب

wheel	عراده	چرخ
wheelchair	تریسایکل	صندلی چرخدار
wheelchair	تریسایکل	ویلچر
whey	قروت	کشک
whirlpool	چرخاب	گرداب
whistle	اشپلاق، شپیلی	سوت
white	ساچی	سفید
white globe	گروپ تباشیری	لامپ مات
whooping cough	سرفه سیاه	سیاه سرفه
wicked	زاغ	مکار
wicket	هوکی	چوگان
wide	کشاد	گشاد
widow	جته	بیوه
wife's brother	خسربره	برادرزن
wife's father	خسر	پدرزن
wife's mother	خشو	مادرزن
wild animals	وحشي ژوي	حیوانات وحشی
wind	شمالک	باد
wind (energy)	باد توری	بادی
window	کلکین	پنجره
wine	واین	شراب
wink	ابروگک	چشمک
wiring	لین دوانی	سیم کشی
womaniser	زنکه باز	خانم باز
women	نسوان	زنان
woodpecker	نجارک	دارکوب
wool scarf	پتو	شال پشمی
work clothes	دریشی کار	لباس کار
worker	اجوره کار، عمله کار	کارگر
workshop	ورکشاپ	تعمیرگاه

worn	داغمه	فرسوده
worn out	از کار افتیده	فرسوده شده
worn-out	تکه تکه	خسته و کوفته
worried	نگران	نگران
wrestler	پهلوان	کشتی گیر
wrist	موسک	مچ
written	تحریری	کتبی

yawn	فاژه	خمیازه
year	کال	سال
yellow	زیر	زرد
yesterday	دینه روز	دیروز
yesterday one	باسی	دیروزی
yoghurt	جغرات، ماست	ماست
yoghurt drink	لسي	دوغ
young	خردترک	خردسال
young woman	پیغله	دوشیزه
zakat (almsgiving)	زکات	زکات
zipper	زپ	زیپ
zone	زون	حوزه
Zoology	ژوولوجستی	جانورشناسی
Zoroastrianism	زرتشتي	زرتشتی

Conclusion

Language is a living thing. It grows, adapts, and changes — shaped by the communities that speak it, the histories they carry, and the worlds they inhabit. Farsi and Dari are proof of this truth. Born from the same ancient roots, nurtured by the same great poets, and written in the same script, they have evolved into two distinct but deeply related expressions of one of humanity's oldest and richest linguistic traditions.

This dictionary has attempted to honour both. By placing English, Dari, and Farsi side by side, it makes visible what is shared and what is different — not to emphasise division, but to build understanding. The translator who knows where the two varieties diverge makes fewer errors. The learner who sees both forms together develops a fuller picture of the language. The community member who recognises the differences between the Persian of Tehran and the Dari of Kabul is better equipped to communicate across the cultural and geographic distance that history has placed between them.

Words matter. The right word, in the right variety, spoken to the right person, can open a door that the wrong word would keep closed. This is not a small thing. In professional translation, in community services, in healthcare, in legal settings, in education, and in the daily work of human connection, the precision that a resource like this dictionary enables has real consequences for real people.

It is also worth saying what this dictionary cannot do. No dictionary captures a language fully. Languages live in voices, in contexts, in the pauses between words and the tones that change meaning. They live in the stories told around fires and the prayers spoken quietly before sleep. They live in the proverbs passed from grandparents to grandchildren and the jokes that only make sense if you grew up in a particular place. A dictionary is a map, not the territory. It points toward the language. The language itself must be found in the people who speak it.

The Persian and Dari languages have survived conquest, displacement, censorship, and centuries of change. They have carried within them the words of Rumi, Hafez, Saadi, and Khayyam — words that have outlasted empires and continue to move readers across the world. They are languages worth knowing, worth preserving, and worth the effort of understanding precisely.

About the Author

Dr Yavar Dehghani is a linguist, educator, and author based in Melbourne, Australia. He holds a PhD in Linguistics and has spent decades working professionally across Persian (Farsi and Dari), Azerbaijani, Turkish, Pashto, and English — languages that between them are spoken by hundreds of millions of people across Central Asia, the Middle East, and their diaspora communities worldwide.

His translation and interpreting work spans legal, medical, educational, and government contexts, where precise understanding of the differences between language varieties — including the differences between Farsi and Dari documented in this dictionary — has direct and significant consequences. This dictionary grew directly out of that professional experience: the recognition that a practical, clearly organised reference documenting the divergences between the two major varieties of Persian was needed and largely unavailable in English.

Dr Dehghani is the author of a wide-ranging catalogue of books covering language learning, cultural studies, mindfulness, migration, wisdom literature, and the philosophy of language. His titles include *Persian (Farsi-Dari) Grammar and Self-Learner*, *Ancient Persian Wisdom for Modern Life*, *Azerbaijani Proverbs and Bayati Poems*, *The Great Minds of Persia*, *The Country You Carry*, and *Questions Humans Are Afraid to Ask*, among others.

All titles are available at yadehghani.com

www.ingramcontent.com/pod-product-compliance
Lightning Source LLC
Chambersburg PA
CBHW012254240726
48655CB00009B/3310